365 CHILDREN'S PRAYERS

Written and compiled by
Carol Watson

Illustrated by
Ann Baum
Steve Gardner
Robert Geary
Annabel Large
Patricia Ludlow
Tony Morris
Avril Turner

A LION BOOK
Oxford . Batavia . Sydney

Copyright © 1989 Lion Publishing
Prayers by the author copyright © 1989 Carol Watson

Published by
Lion Publishing plc
Sandy Lane West, Littlemore, Oxford, England
ISBN 0 7459 1454 3
ISBN 0 7459 1721 6 (Gift edition)
Lion Publishing Corporation
1705 Hubbard Avenue, Batavia, Illinois 60510, USA
ISBN 0 7459 1454 3
ISBN 0 7459 1721 6 (Gift edition)
Albatross Books Pty Ltd
PO Box 320, Sutherland, NSW 2232, Australia
ISBN 0 7324 0010 4

First edition 1989
Reprinted 1989

The author would like to thank the following for their help
and support in the making of this book:

The children and teachers of the Sunday schools at these
churches:
  Holy Trinity, Brompton, London SW7
  St Barnabas, Addison Gardens, London W14

The children and teachers of:
  The King's School, Witney, Oxford
  St Mary's Church of England Middle School,
  Puddletown, Dorset
  St Christina's School, St John's Wood, London
  Strand on the Green Primary School, Chiswick, London
  St Anthony's Convent Preparatory School, Westbury,
  Dorset
  Southill County Primary School, Weymouth, Dorset

With special thanks to Michael Ellis, His Honour
Judge Christopher Compston, Rachel Tingle,
John Bazlinton, Joan Murray-Brown, Prudence Lynch,
Dr Tony Potter, Diana McGuiness and Lydia Fetto.

British Library Cataloguing in Publication Data
365 children's prayers.
  1. Children. Christian life. Prayer—
Collections
I. Watson, Carol
242'.82
  ISBN 0–7459–1454–3

Library of Congress Cataloging in Publication Data
365 children's prayers/compiled by Carol Watson. — 1st ed.
    "A Lion book."
  ISBN 0–7459–1454–3
  1. Children—Prayer-books and devotions—English.
[1. Prayers. 2. Prayer books and devotions.]
I. Watson, Carol. II. Title: Three hundred and sixty-five
children's prayers.

Printed in Yugoslavia

365
CHILDREN'S
PRAYERS

For my godchildren
Angela, Chloë, Joseph,
Edward and India

CONTENTS

INTRODUCTION

Do you ever talk to God, or pray? What sort of things do you pray about? Is praying something you do only on Sundays or at night when you go to bed? Some of us only pray when we are in trouble or danger, but we can pray to God at any time or in any place. God wants us to talk to him about everything.

There are different kinds of prayer. Sometimes we want to praise God for the wonderful things in the world or to thank him for what he has done for us. At other times we may like to pray on behalf of someone else, asking God to help or care for them. We often need to ask God's forgiveness or just talk out our worries and fears. There are also times when we just simply feel like worshipping God for all his goodness.

In this book you will find prayers grouped together under themes. They begin with home, school and everyday experiences and then move out to cover wider issues of the world, other people and our different feelings. Well-loved and traditional prayers are combined with new and topical ones, and there are also many prayers recently written by children.

The best prayers are often the ones we say naturally when we're happy, excited or worried about something. But sometimes we find it easier to say prayers which have been written for us. You can say the prayers in this book on your own, or read them with your parents or teachers, at any time and in any situation where they help you come close to God and his love.

Carol Watson

Our Own World

Me

Lord . . . you know me and everything I do.
Psalm 139:1-2

1 Dear God,
you know all about me;
you know how I feel, when I'm happy or sad;
you know what I say, when I'm kind or rude;
you know what I do, when I'm good or bad.
Dear God,
thank you for knowing all about me
and still loving me.

2 Make me pure, Lord: thou art holy;
Make me meek, Lord: thou wert lowly.

Gerard Manley Hopkins (1844–89)

3 Thank you, God, for making me.
Thank you that you made me how I am.
Thank you for my talents and weaknesses.
Thank you for all my friends.
Most of all, thank you for making me a child for you.
Amen

Matthew Biddlecombe (aged 11)

4 You know what I am thinking, Lord.
You know what is best for me.
Whatever happens, I want to please you.
Amen

5 God be in my head,
And in my understanding;
God be in my eyes,
And in my looking;
God be in my mouth
And in my speaking;
God be in my heart,
And in my thinking;
God be at my end,
And at my departing.

16th-century Sarum Primer

6 Dear Lord,
You know I am not perfect. If you're a Christian you're
still not perfect. Please help me.
Amen

Edward Lawson-Johnson (aged 8)

7 Christ be with me
Christ within me
Christ behind me
Christ before me
Christ beside me
Christ to win me
Christ to comfort and restore me
Christ beneath me
Christ above me
Christ in quiet and
Christ in danger
Christ in hearts of all that love me
Christ in mouth of friend and stranger.

St Patrick (389–461)

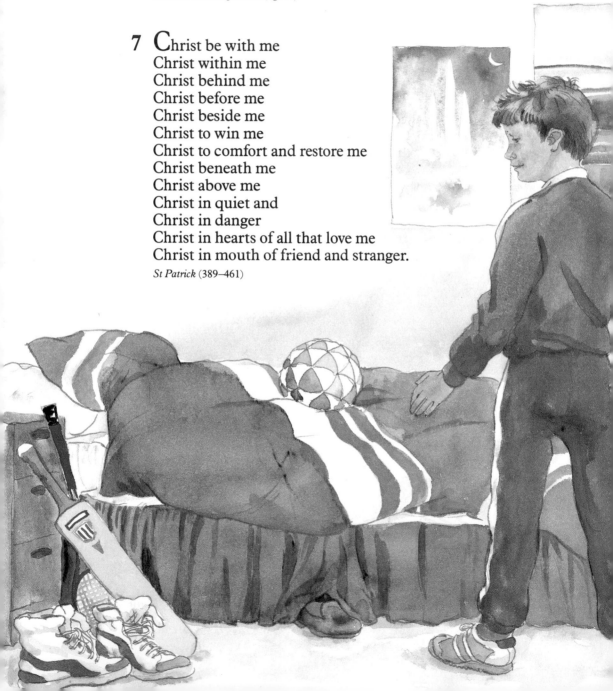

8 Lord, I thank you for making me.
Thank you for all that I can do.
Thank you that I can run, jump, and play games.
Thank you that I can listen to what you tell me.
Thank you that you love me whatever I do.

Andrew (aged 12)

9 O God, give me in my life the fruit of peace.
Help me to take things calmly.
Help me not to get into a panic when things go wrong.
Help me not to worry but to take things as they come,
a day at a time.
Help me not to be nervous but to keep cool when I have
something important to do.
Help me never to lose my temper, no matter how
annoying things or people may be.
Keep me calm and steady, so that I will never collapse,
and so that others may be able to rely on me when
they are up against it.
This I ask for Jesus' sake, Amen

10 Thank you, Lord, that even though I'm not perfect
and have my failures, nothing and no one can change
the fact that you love me — just as I am.

Tammy Williams (aged 13)

In the Morning

In the morning will I direct my prayer to you.
Psalm 5:3

11 Lord, be with us this day.
Within us to purify us;
Above us to draw us up;
Beneath us to sustain us;
Before us to lead us;
Behind us to restrain us;
Around us to protect us.

St Patrick (389–461)

12 Now another day is breaking,
Sleep was sweet and so is waking,
Dear Lord, I promised you last night
Never again to sulk or fight.
Such vows are easier to keep
When a child is sound asleep.
Today, O Lord, for your dear sake,
I'll try to keep them when awake.

Ogden Nash

13 Dear Father, as we start this day,
please will you help us.
Please help Mum and Dad as they work.
Please help me at school.
Please help my little sister at home,
And all my other friends and family.
Amen

14 Father God,
Thank you for sleep and bringing us safely through
another night.
Thank you for a new morning and for health and
energy to tackle the day.
Lord, be with us throughout this day as we eat and
work and play.
Fill us with your love for everything and everyone
around us.
Amen

15 For this new morning and its light,
For rest and shelter of the night,
For health and food, for love and friends,
For every gift your goodness sends,
We thank you, gracious Lord.

Anon

16 Let this day, O Lord, add some knowledge or good
deed to yesterday.

Lancelot Andrewes (1555–1626)

17 Thy steadfast love, O Lord, never ceases,
Thy mercies never come to an end;
They are new each morning;
Great is thy faithfulness.

Lamentations 3:22-23

18 Into thy hands, O Lord, we commit ourselves this day.
Give to each one of us a watchful, a humble, and a
diligent spirit, that we may seek in all things to know
thy will, and when we know it may perform it perfectly
and gladly, to the honour and glory of thy name,
through Jesus Christ our Lord.

5th-century Gelasian Sacramentary

19 O God, all through today help me:
Not to lose my temper even when people and things
annoy me.
Not to lose my patience even when things do not
come out right the first time;
Not to lose my hope when things are difficult and
when learning is hard;
Not to lose my goodness and honour, even when I am
tempted to take the wrong way.
Help me so to live today that I will have nothing to be
sorry for when I go to bed again at night.
Hear this my prayer for Jesus' sake.
Amen

20 Direct, control, suggest, this day,
All I design, or do, or say,
That all my powers, with all their might,
In thy sole glory may unite.

Bishop Thomas Ken (1637–1711)

Our Families

Honour your father and your mother . . .
Exodus 20:12

21 Thank you, dear heavenly Father, for making us part of your family. It is good to know that we belong to you, and to each other as brothers and sisters. Please teach us to love one another however difficult it may seem, and to care for those who are in your family and live in countries where they have very little to eat and maybe nowhere to live. Help us to share things with them as we would with our own family.
For Jesus' sake, Amen

22 Dear God,
Please look after everyone in my family
Protect them from harm — keep them healthy
and give them your peace.
Amen

23 Dear Lord,
Please take care of my auntie
because she is having a baby.
P.S. Make it a boy, *please.*

Julian Parmiter (aged 11)

24 Father God,
My dad works very hard.
Sometimes he has to work nights and
we hardly see him at all.
Help me to be good when he's around
to make his life easier.
Amen

25 God,
you know that now and then
I have a hard time
getting along with my mum.
Sometimes she doesn't understand me,
and I don't understand her either.
Yet today
she was really kind of nice,
not nagging,
just nice!
Thank you, God.

26 Dear Lord,
Today, my baby brother came home from hospital.
He is very small and cries a lot. Please help him to
grow up quickly so that I can play with him.

27 Lord Jesus,
My mum went away.
Where is she?
I miss her, Lord, and so does my dad.
Sometimes he cries at night when he thinks we're
all asleep.
Wherever she is, Lord, keep her safe and love her.
Give my dad some extra love because he needs it
just now.
Amen

28 Please, Lord, bless all the children who don't have a
mother or father — and those who may even have no
family at all. You know what they are feeling and how
much love they need. Father, you love us *all*. Give more
love than ever to these children now. Heal their hurts
and ease their pain.
In Jesus' name,
Amen

29 Lord Jesus,
Sometimes I feel no one listens.
Dad is working, Mum is busy — everyone has
things to do. There is no one to really *hear* me.
But you do, Lord. You are always there.
Thank you.
Amen

30 Thank you, Lord, for Granny and Grandpa.
Please look after them as they get old.

31 Forgive us, heavenly Father, when anger and
bickering disturb the peace of our family. Help
us always to find the right words of love and
encouragement and to do the right thing to soothe and
heal the hurt. Forgive us when we quarrel. Help us to
smile more often. Help us to forgive others and help
others to forgive us.
Through Jesus Christ our Lord, Amen

32 Lord, I pray for my mum today — that you'd give her
the strength to get through the day. Please help her
forget she overslept this morning.
Ruth Dillon (aged 11)

33 Jesus, when you were in all that pain on the cross,
you still thought of your mother, Mary.
Please help me to look after my mum.

39 Father God,
Homes are not always happy and loving.
Sometimes there is fighting and shouting, arguments
and anger.
There are times when we might not want to go home
at all — but we may be too ashamed to tell anyone how
we feel.
Lord, you know all our worries and problems.
Help us to pray to you about the things which trouble
us and to know that whatever happens you are always
there, loving us.

40 Jesus,
I thank you for my home — and that when it's winter,
we can keep warm inside our house.
Amen

Ruth Dillon (aged 11)

41 Our dear Lord,
Thank you for bringing me to this children's home.
Before I didn't know you, and I always quarrelled
and took away things which were not mine.
I was lazy.
Now I don't do it any more because you told me in
your book, the Bible.
I am now happy.
Thank you Lord.

A child's prayer from the Philippines

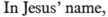

42 Dear Lord Jesus,
When you came into the world you had no home —
your bed was a manger and your shelter, a stable.
Help us to remember all the people in this country
and all over the world who are homeless today.
Help us to think of what we can do for them.
Make us more caring and loving to those who have
no place to stay.
Amen

43 Father,
Bless all those children who are frightened at home —
afraid of someone there who treats them badly.
Help them to remember that you know everything that
happens and that you love them.
Give them the courage to speak out to caring people
who can help them.
Touch their hearts and minds with your love and heal
the hurt and suffering.
In Jesus' name,
Amen

Our Food

Give thanks to the Lord . . . who gives food to every creature.
Psalm 136:1,25

44 For my daily food, I thank you, Lord.
For the farmers, shopkeepers and cooks who prepare
my food, I thank you, Lord.
For my favourite foods, I thank you, Lord.
Help us to care about people not having enough food.
Amen

45 Blessed art thou, O Lord our God, King of the
universe, who bringest forth bread from the earth.
A Jewish blessing

46 Father,
We pray for those in lands where there is famine and misery. Lord, some children have never known what it is like to eat proper meals as we do. Their lives will not get better unless those of us who have money and food help them.
Lord Jesus, please make us more loving and giving — help us to think what we can do for the hungry, and give us the determination *to do it*.
In Jesus' name, Amen

47 My God, I thank you for my food.
It is you that allows the rice,
the beans, the wheat, the fruit,
the animals and the vegetables to grow.
I thank you for the food
that is on the table.
Thank you very much, Lord.

A child's prayer from Brazil

48 Lord, I have this problem with chocolate — I can't stop eating it — although I know it rots my teeth and gives me spots. Please help me to resist things which I know are bad for me.
Amen

49 Dear Lord Jesus, I'm sorry.
Sometimes I think about food too much.
I dream of all the delicious things there are to eat when I really should be doing other things.
Please help me not to make food so important, and help me not to be greedy at mealtimes.
Amen

50 For water ices, cheap but good,
That find us in a thirsty mood;
For ices made of milk or cream
That slip down smoothly as a dream;
For cornets, sandwiches and pies
That make the gastric juices rise;
For ices bought in little shops
Or at the kerb from him who stops;
For chanting of the sweet refrain:
'Vanilla, strawberry or plain?'
We thank thee, Lord, who sends with the heat
This cool deliciousness to eat.

51 Dear God,
Please help all the neglected people in the world who
can't just go into the kitchen and get a sandwich.

A child's prayer from Australia

52 Lord,
Thank you that every day we have good things to eat.
Help us to appreciate what we have and try not to be
fussy or wasteful.
Amen

53 Fruit and nuts and berries,
Growing ripe and sweet,
Vegetables and golden corn
All for us to eat.

Rich food in its plenty,
Picked and stored away,
While others in their countries
Are starving every day.

Mothers in the market,
Choosing what to eat,
Perhaps a rich fruit pudding
For a special treat.

In heats of Ethiopia,
Little grows on land.
A mother looks at the food for the day
Which only fills one hand.

In lands of drought and hunger
No more, dear Lord, we pray
Will mothers ask the question
Which child to feed today?

James Anthony Carey (aged 10)

60 Forgive me, Lord Jesus, today I felt jealous and angry. I said things which were spiteful and unkind. Help me to say I'm sorry and make things better.

61 Dear Lord,
Bless those who are lonely and have no friends. Help us to talk to others we sometimes find difficult, strange or shy. Let our friendship help them to come to know you and your love.
Amen

62 Help me, O God, to be a good and true friend:
To be always loyal, and never to let my friends down;
Never to talk about them behind their backs in a way
I would not do before their faces;
Never to betray a confidence or talk about the things
about which I ought to be silent;
Always to be ready to share everything I have:
To be as true to my friends as I would wish them to be
to me.
This I ask for the sake of him who is the greatest and
the truest of all friends, for Jesus' sake. Amen

63 Dear Jesus,
My friend moved house last week.
She's gone to live far away with her mum and dad.
I miss her Lord, and she misses me.
Help us to make new friends quickly
so we won't be so sad.
Thank you.
Amen

Our Pets

All kinds of animals, birds, reptiles and creatures of the sea . . .
have been tamed by man.
James 3:7

64 I love my cat —
her gentle purring,
the softness of her fur,
her funny face
and curious nature.
Thank you for making her, Lord, and for all pets.
Thank you for all the different things about
them that we love.

65 Dear Lord Jesus, our little dog has died. We cried
because she was so loving and good. She made
everyone happy. We are glad it's you who've got her
now. Please take care of her, but of course you will.
You love all animals. You made them all. Thank you
for letting us have her first and for all the happy
times we've had with her.

66 Dear Lord,
Please make sure my hamster is happy.
As he can't talk to me I can't be sure.
Also, please help me to look after him
better — I keep forgetting.
Lois Potter (aged 11)

67 Thank you, God, for animals.
Thank you that you gave us them to enjoy.
Help us to look after them.
Thank you especially for our pets.
Help us to care for them and love them.
Amen
Derek Hobbs (aged 10)

68 He prayeth best, who loveth best
All things both great and small;
For the dear God who loveth us,
He made and loveth all.

S. T. Coleridge (1772–1834)

At School

Whatever you do, work at it with all your heart . . .
Colossians 3:23

69 Dear God, I'm scared.
I've seen the big school.
We went last term to look round.
But you know what it's like, anyway.
There are big boys there.
We were the biggest in our school.
It's going to feel strange.
The teachers aren't like ours.
We'll be having lots of them.
We have to go to different rooms
all round the school.
I'm frightened I'll get lost.
There's corridors all over the place, Lord.
I suppose you know all about that too.
Help me to find somebody to show me the ropes.
Please let me feel like I belong
to this new school.
After all, it's my school now.

70 Thank you, Lord, for school.
Thank you that it teaches you to do things.
Lord, please help me to do the best I can in every single
way.
Amen

Naomi Nicholson (aged 11)

71 Lord,
Help me with my work. I'm not very clever, but I try.
It's embarrassing not getting good marks — people
laughing; people saying 'you're thick!'
I'm getting better, but with your help I could be the
best!

J. Powers (aged 12)

72 The things, good Lord, that we pray for,
give us grace to work for;
through Jesus Christ our Lord.

Sir Thomas More (1478–1535)

73 Father God, help us in our work each day. Give us
concentration so that we may listen, understanding
that we may learn, and peaceful minds so that we may
remember.
In Jesus' name,
Amen

74 Dear Lord Jesus,
Thank you for helping me through this term at school.
I pray that the holidays are a refreshing rest. Please let
next term be better than the last one.

Anna Campbell (aged 9)

75 I do not ask, O Lord, that you will think my thoughts for me or do my work for me, but that you will help me: so that what is too hard for me to do alone, and what is too difficult for me to understand by myself, I may be able to do and understand because you are with me. Teach me to think of Jesus as my friend and as one who is always by my side, for his name's sake.

76 Thank you, God, for friends because I like to play; and thank you for teachers because if we didn't have teachers we wouldn't learn as much.
I love you, Lord.
Amen

Adam Russell (aged 8)

77 Dear Lord Jesus,
Thank you for the work we have done today,
For the exercise it has given our minds;
For the pleasure we have had from it.
Help us always to enjoy our work, whatever it is, and to do it with all our hearts to your praise and glory.
Please bless those who have no work especially if they have had none for a long time.
They must be very bored and unhappy.
Please help their families to help them and give them some work to do soon.

78 Thank you for our school and for everyone who
works here.
Thank you for the teachers who help us to learn,
for the people who give us our food,
for the cleaners who clear up after us
and for the caretaker who watches over the school and
keeps it safe.
Thank you that we can go to school each day, and that
we are more fortunate than many children elsewhere in
the world who have no schools to go to and cannot have
an education.
In Jesus' name,
Amen

Our Church

You are . . . God's own people.
1 Peter 2:9

79 Thank you for churches, God.
They mean we can talk to you more often
and discuss our problems together
and pray to you.

Steven Hadley (aged 9)

80 Lord, when we think of 'the church',
we think of our own building,
our own friends,
those who worship with us now.
Lord, when *you* see the church,
you see Christians in every century,
your people spread throughout the world,
stretching through time.
Lord, help us to see how great the church is;
and to be glad that we belong to your family.

81 Peacefulness lingers in the air.
Soft footsteps of people,
Quiet voices.
Echoes of
Prayer
Praise
Worship
Trapped in the walls — caught in the arches.

Jasmine Threlfall (aged 10)

82 Father God,
Thank you for the church and all the teachers.
Thank you that they help us to learn about you.
Please help us to remember what we are taught
and help us to put it into practice.
Amen

Alex Foote (aged 12)

83 Lord,
We want to fill our churches with people who worship
and praise you. We want everyone to know the joy of
your love.
Please God, give us the courage to tell our friends
about you. Help us to overcome our shyness.
In the world today we are sometimes made to feel
embarrassed about being Christians.
Help us to speak out more about you and your love,
and not to worry about what others might think.
In Jesus' name,
Amen

That's Fun!

A happy heart makes the face cheerful . . .
Proverbs 15:13

88 Lord, thank you for television!
It can entertain us and make us laugh.
It can bring to us people and places from all over
the world.
It can give us ideas for things to do and make.
Lord, help us to choose the programmes we watch,
to help us to know more of your world.

89 Thank you, God, for actors and ballerinas.
Please help them, they must get very tired.
Thank you for entertainment.
Amen

Nadine Nicolson (aged 8)

90 Big books and paperbacks:
novels and histories and plays;
romance and tragedy;
cartoons and picture books;
serious and fun;
borrowed and bought;
books and comics.
Thank you, God for books and the gift of reading.

91 Living Lord,
thank you for our hobbies,
and the different things we enjoy.
Thank you for the interest of building up a collection;
thank you for the joy of stretching our bodies in sports;
thank you for the satisfaction of making things.
We praise you for the things we do alone,
that are special to us,
and for the fun of working together.
Thank you, Lord, for those who teach us and help us,
for those who give us new ideas.
Lord, there is so much to discover and enjoy —
thank you!

92 Thank you, Lord,
for everyone who helps us to enjoy ourselves;
for people who make the television programmes
I watch;
for people who produce the records I listen to;
for people who write books and illustrate them;
for people who invent toys and games.
Thank you, Lord,
for everyone who helps us to enjoy ourselves.

Music and Song

They celebrated joyfully . . .
with songs . . . and with the music of cymbals, harps and lyres.
Nehemiah 12:27

93 Lord, thank you for giving us music and for the great composers and musicians. Thank you for giving us the technology to hear the music at any time from radios and stereos. Thank you for sad music, happy music and funny music.
Amen

Sarah Fudge (aged 10)

94 Holy, holy, holy, Lord God Almighty!
Early in the morning our song shall rise to thee.

Bishop Herbert (1782–1826)

95 Lord, we praise you for the joy of music, and the skill of those who compose or play it.
We do not all like the same kind of music, but there is so much variety that we can all find something to delight our ears.
We thank you for songs which we can sing.
We thank you that we can use music in our worship.
We thank you for musicians who give pleasure to so many.
Accept our thanks, we pray.

96 Thank you, God,
that we can sing to you and praise you.
Thank you because music is fun and
we can sing nice songs.
Amen

Hannah Biddlecombe (aged 8)

97 Father God, it is sometimes just fantastic to play
music really loudly and to dance and sing. It makes us
feel so good. But help us to remember that this may
disturb our family or neighbours. Help us to find the
right time and place to enjoy ourselves and not to forget
others who may be wanting some peace.
In Jesus' name,
Amen

Sport and Games

Physical training is of some value, but godliness has value for all things . . .
1 Timothy 4:8

98 Thank you, Lord, that we can run and jump.
Thank you that we can dive and swim.
Thank you for designing our bodies so that we can play
all kinds of games.
Thank you for the good feelings we have when we have
exercised well.
Help us to keep our bodies fit and healthy.
In Jesus' name,
Amen

99 Dear God,
Thank you for the sports that we play and for our
country's great sportsmen and women. Please bless
and help everybody in the Olympic Games.
Craig Burton (aged 9)

100 O God,
We pray thee, help us to run a straight race through
thy good grace. May we compete against others in
friendly rivalry, accept defeat and success humbly, and
always play fair.

101 Dear Jesus,
Help us to be good sportsmen and sportswomen.
If we lose, help us to lose graciously — and please
help us not to get injured.
Stephen Matthews (aged 13)

102 Dear God,
Thank you for the fields we play on.
Thank you, Lord, for high jump.
Amen
Colin Sell (aged 9)

Health and Fitness

May you enjoy good health and may all go well with you.
3 John :2

103 Lord,
I want to thank you
for all the medicines we have
that help cure diseases.
Yet there's an uneasiness inside
that won't go away.
I hear about teenagers
who are turning on with drugs
and it bothers me, Lord.
I need you here.
Help me
if others ask me to try things.
Give me strength to say no
and no
and no again.
Remind me
that I don't need something
to put me down
or build me up,
that the power
you have given me
helps me live
just the way
I am.

104 Please Father God,
Bless those who do not have good health.
Strengthen them and give them patience.
Let them know your love is always there
when they are feeling low.
Amen

105 Dear Lord,
Everyone around me is always smoking. I know it's
bad to do this, but I find it really hard. So, could you
give me the strength not to do such things, and help
other people to give it up.

Andrew Goddard (aged 15)

106 O God, bless and help all those who have to face
life with some handicap.
Those who are lame and crippled, who cannot run
and jump and play the games which other people play;
Those who are blind and who cannot see the light of
the sun or the faces of their dear friends;
Those who are deaf, who cannot hear the voices of
their friends, who cannot listen to the music or the
singing of the birds;
Those whose minds are disturbed and for whom the
kindly light of reason burns dim;
Those who find learning difficult, and for whom it
is a constant struggle to keep up with the class.
Give courage and strength and help to all those who
are handicapped, and grant that those who are strong
may be ever ready and willing to help them;
through Jesus Christ our Lord,
Amen

At Night

I will lie down and sleep in peace, for you alone,
O Lord, make me dwell in safety.
Psalm 4:8

107 The night is come, like to the day;
Depart not thou, great God, away . . .
Guard me 'gainst those watchful foes,
Whose eyes are open while mine close.

Sir Thomas Browne (1643)

108 Father God,
Sometimes in the night I am frightened.
I think I can see monsters and shadowy people in the
dark. I hear the stairs creak and strange night noises.
Lord, help me to remember that you are always there
with me and I need not be afraid.
Amen

109 From ghoulies and ghosties,
Long-leggety beasties,
And things that go bump in the night,
Good Lord deliver us.

Traditional

110 Hush! my dear, lie still and slumber,
Holy angels guard thy bed!
Heavenly blessings without number
Gently falling on thy head.

Sleep, my babe; thy food and raiment,
House and home, thy friends provide;
All without thy care or payment,
All thy wants are well supplied.

How much better thou'rt attended
Than the Son of God could be,
When from heaven he descended
And became a child like thee!

Soft and easy is thy cradle:
Coarse and hard thy Saviour lay:
When his birthplace was a stable,
And his softest bed was hay.

Isaac Watts (1674–1748)

111 Father,
Thank you for all the good things
that have happened today.
Thank you for keeping me safe and well,
Thank you for fun and laughter with my friends,
Thank you for what I have learned,
Thank you for all those that I love.
Help us all to sleep soundly tonight.
Amen

112 Good night! Good night!
Far flies the light;
But still God's love
Shall flame above,
Making all bright.
Good night! Good night!

Victor Hugo

113 Lord Jesus,
This night forgive me for all that I have done wrong
throughout today. I am sorry if I have been rude,
disobedient, or unhelpful. Sometimes it's difficult to
be good all the time. Help me to do better tomorrow.
Amen

114 Watch thou, dear Lord, with those who wake or
watch or weep tonight, and give thine angels charge
over those who sleep.
Tend thy sick ones, O Lord Christ, rest thy weary ones.
Bless thy dying ones. Shield thy joyous ones.
And all for thy love's sake.

St Augustine (354–430)

115 Dear Lord, why does everything seem so much worse
in the dark? When I wake up in the night my worries
seem to grow and grow.
Then I remember that you are there with your love.
I feel your peace calming me and I sleep once again.

116 The moon shines bright,
The stars give light
Before the break of day;
God bless you all
Both great and small
And send a joyful day.

Traditional

Feelings and Attitudes

Loving Others

God is love. Whoever lives in love lives in God, and God in him.
1 John 4:16

117 Lord, help us to remember that:
'Love is patient, love is kind. It does not envy, it does
not boast, it is not proud. It is not rude, it is not self-
seeking, it is not easily angered, it keeps no record of
wrongs. Love does not delight in evil but rejoices with
the truth. It always protects, always trusts, always
hopes, always perseveres. Love never fails.'
From 1 Corinthians 13

118 Lord Jesus, you say in the Bible, 'greater love has no one than that he lay down his life for his friends'. You laid down your life for us so that we could be forgiven for all that we have done wrong and could become your friends. Thank you for showing us such a great love.
In your name,
Amen

119 Dear Father God,
When I pray to you I feel warm and happy inside.
It's like the love that I feel for my mum and dad when I hug them at night.
Thank you for loving feelings.

120 Lord, I know
That one of the best ways I can show
my love for you is by loving other people.
Sometimes this is easy —
when I'm with people I like.

Please help me when loving is hard,
when people are unkind,
when I don't understand,
when I just don't like them.

Teach me to love as you loved
when you were walking about in Palestine.
Teach me to love as you love now —
Everyone
Always.

121 O Lord, give us, we beseech thee, in the name of Jesus Christ, that love which shall never cease, that will kindle our lamps but not extinguish them, that they may enlighten others and may always desire thee.

St Columba (521–97)

122 Lord, you have created us with love and for love. We are sorry for the hatred in the world and in our hearts. You endured the cross for love of us and to conquer hate. Help us to grow in love.
Amen

123 Father, I'm really not good at loving my enemies —
people who laugh at me and make fun of me behind my
back — the guys who beat me up in the playground
and call me names in the street. My heart gets filled up
with anger and hate and there isn't much room left for
love. Lord, help me to keep away the bad feelings; help
me to love everyone no matter what they do.

124 Dear God,
Thank you that you love children.
Thank you that yours is a very special love;
you love us even more than a father loves his own
children, because you made us and we belong to you.
Thank you, God,
Amen

125 Father God,
There are lots of people who never feel loving and some
who don't have anyone at all to love them. Help them
to know that you are always there with your love — if
they would only turn to you.
In Jesus' name,
Amen

126 God bless all those that I love;
God bless all those that love me;
God bless all those that love those that I love,
And all those that love those that love me.

From an old New England sampler

Feeling Frightened

I will not be afraid, Lord, for you are with me.
Psalm 23:4

127 Please give me courage, Lord. I'm frightened of so many things that people would call me a coward if they knew. I've never dared let anyone know how scared I am of being out alone in the dark. I'm afraid of burglars, afraid of storms and of getting hurt, or of anyone I love being injured or taken ill. I wouldn't dare tell anyone but you about all this. Please God, help me not to be so afraid and give me courage to face whatever comes.

128 Lord, I thank you that when we are frightened we can turn to you for help. I thank you that you have your hand over us all the time and you comfort us.
Amen

Paul Nadin (aged 11)

129 Please Lord,
Help me to be brave and strong in you,
and take my fear away.
Amen

Stephen Matthews (aged 13)

130 Alone with none but thee, my God,
I journey on my way.
What need I fear, when thou art near
O King of night and day?
More safe am I within thy hand
Than if a host did round me stand.

St Columba (521–97)

131 Dear Jesus,
Please stop the butterflies in my tummy which come
when I have to do something hard. Give me the right
words at the right time. Please guide me through the
whole day.
Thank you.
Amen

132 Thank you, Lord, that you are with us when we are feeling frightened and that you help us through it, so that when we have finished praying to you we feel happy and full of joy. It's as if you've come along with your magnet and taken away the frightened feeling. Amen

David Rapson (aged 13)

133 He who would valiant be
'Gainst all disaster
Let him in constancy
Follow the Master.

John Bunyan (1628–88)

134 Thank you, Lord, that you reach deep, deep down
into my heart to take care and heal all my worries
and hurts.

Susanna Llewellyn (aged 12)

135 Jesus, when I am afraid, help me to remember that
you are with me, nearer than my breathing, closer than
my beating heart. You understand my fears better than
I do, so let me trust in you and give me the grace to
support others in their fears as you support me.
Amen

136 Heavenly Father,
I thank you that you have not given me the spirit of
fear, but of power and love. I let the peace of God rule
in my heart — I trust in you, Lord, and you show me
the way I should go.

137 There is nothing to fear
For God is here
He never will leave me
Or forsake me
God is with me.

God is with me
Every day
So I have no need to dismay
He protects me in every way
And I praise him.

Simon Dillon (aged 12)

Feeling Lonely

Jesus said: 'I will be with you always, to the very end of the age.'
Matthew 28:20

138 I'm lonely, Lord.
I don't feel loved.
There's a noise around me,
often there's a crowd.
I stand in the middle of the crowd
and I look around,
and I feel as though
I'm standing there
alone.
Isn't there a human being
who can take my loneliness away?
Someone who can reach out
and make me feel
that I belong?
I'm lonely, Lord.
I need your love.
I need the love
you gave when you died for me.
I need your love
because it's there for ever.
Thank you, Lord!

139 Father God,
There are so many lonely people in the world.
Some of them are our neighbours — some are children
at school. Often we don't notice how lonely they
are. Help us to look out for anyone who may need
friendship and think what we can do for them.
In Jesus' name,
Amen

140 Dear Lord,
Please help me when I am feeling lonely. Help me
when I'm sad after the people at school tease me.
Please let everyone get along in this world.

Tom Hetherington (aged 10)

141 O Lord, never suffer us to think that we can stand by
ourselves, and not need thee.

John Donne (1573–1631)

142 Father God,
I feel lonely and left out. Thank you that you haven't
left me out. You promise always to remember me and
never forsake me. Thank you that I am important to
you but please help me to learn, too, how to let others
come in front of me.

When We Are Ill

I will bind up the injured and strengthen the weak . . .
Ezekiel 34:16

143 Dear Father God,
Today there are many children all over the world who
cannot get up because they are sick. Some of them have
been ill for a long time and have forgotten what it is like
to run and play and enjoy games with their friends.
Lord, help us to imagine what it is like to have to stay
in bed all the time, and how lonely it must feel. Help us
to think what we can do for anyone *we* know who is ill.
In Jesus' name,
Amen

144 Lord Jesus, I am ill.
Please make me well.
Help me to be brave,
and thankful to the people
looking after me.
Thank you for being here with me.

145 Dear Lord,
It is really horrible seeing my friend ill.
I pray that you'll make her better so that we can play
together again.
Amen

Anna Campbell (aged 9)

146 Lord, we want to pray today for those people who we
know are sick and in hospital. We ask that today each
one of them would be aware of your love for them, and
that they would turn to you for strength to face their
sickness. Help them not to be unhappy because they
are unwell, but to learn something special about you
during this time . . .
In Jesus' name,
Amen

147 Dear God, please, please make my friend get well.
Help the doctors invent new medicines that will make
him better.
Amen

Edward Bowring (aged 7)

148 Dear Lord Jesus,
I don't feel well.
My head hurts and my eyes are hot and prickly.
I feel a bit like crying.
Please Lord, be with me now — I need your love.

Caring and Sharing

The Son of Man did not come to be served, but to serve . . .
Mark 10:45

149 Father, sometimes we care about ourselves more than we care about others. We have worries and problems which fill up our minds. Help us, Lord, to remember those who may need our love and help — our families, friends and people we meet every day. Teach us to be more giving and to care for everyone as you do.
In Jesus' name,
Amen

150 Little deeds of kindness,
Little words of love,
Help to make earth happy,
Like the heaven above.

Julia Carney (1823–1908)

151 Thank you, God, for your gift of caring
and your gift of giving.
Thank you that you care for us.
I pray that you would help us to care more.
Amen

Ruth Elmitt (aged 8)

152 Lord, I'm sorry for the times when I'm not
very helpful:
I leave my clothes and toys all over the floor;
I forget to take off my muddy boots and shoes;
I spill my drinks and paints on the furniture;
I make a noise when other people want me to
be quiet.
Lord, please make me more helpful every day.

153 Dear Lord, my granny can't get around much any
more. Her legs hurt when she walks and she needs
people to visit her all the time. Lord Jesus, make me
more thoughtful and caring — let me remember to help
her more often and to make things easier for her.
Amen

154 Make us ever eager, Lord, to share the good things that we have. Grant us such a measure of thy Spirit that we may find more joy in giving than in getting. Make us ready to give cheerfully without grudging, secretly without praise, and in sincerity without looking for gratitude, for Jesus Christ's sake.

John Hunter (1849–1917)

155 Can I see another's woe,
And not be in sorrow too?
Can I see another's grief,
And not seek for kind relief?

William Blake (1757–1827)

156 Thank you, Lord, that you care for us
and give us what we need so that we can live.
Amen

Tracey-Anne Braye (aged 12)

157 O Divine Master,
grant that I may not so much seek
to be consoled, as to console,
to be understood, as to understand,
to be loved, as to love;
for it is in giving that we receive . . .

St Francis of Assisi (1182–1226)

158 Father God,
You have given us all different skills and talents. Some
of us have more money than others; some, more time.
Whatever it is that we have, dear Lord, help us to use it
in a caring way for the service of others — and so in
serving them we can show our love for you.
In Jesus' name,
Amen

When Someone Dies

God gives us the victory over death through our Lord Jesus Christ.
1 Corinthians 15:57

159 Dear Lord Jesus, you cried when your friend Lazarus died, so you understand how we are feeling today. Comfort us as we are sad and lonely without the one we loved so much.
Help us to be glad that our friend is happy with you and free for ever from sadness and pain. Teach us to trust and love you so that we too may live with you for ever.

160 Dear God,
Please could you look after my cat which died a few months ago.
Amen

Thomas Loasby (aged 9)

161 Lord, it's hard for us when those we love die. But there is a place for your friends in heaven and they will be much happier there than any place on earth, because you will be there. Thank you that we will also be with you, the Father, one day.
Amen

James Hill (aged 12)

162 Dear Lord,
Why do people have to die?
I know that they live in heaven after death on earth, but why can't they live for ever on earth?
Lord Jesus Christ, please let me live a long life, and let me see my relatives when I die.
Amen

Simon Penny (aged 10)

163 Dear Father God,
I know that we all have to die sometime.
Everything dies eventually.
Thank you that when I die I will be with you.
Thank you that when we know you we can be happy when we die.
But Lord, it is not easy to be happy when someone *we* love dies.
It takes a long time to stop the aching in our hearts, and to fill up the emptiness left behind.
Lord God, strengthen us with your love when we lose those that we love.
In Jesus' name,
Amen

Feeling Angry

A gentle answer turns away wrath, but a harsh word stirs up anger.
Proverbs 15:1

164 Dear Lord,
Sometimes I feel angry. Please help me to calm my feelings. Lord, forgive me, because sometimes I feel angry with you, too.
Amen

Colin Hillier (aged 9)

165 Father God,
I often resent what I am made to do.
I hate having to say 'all right' when I really feel
like saying 'no!'

Andrew (aged 15)

166 I've had a row with my friend.
We said terrible things and
were full of anger and pride.
Now I feel hurt.
I want to say I'm sorry — but why should I be first?
I want everything to be right again.
Perhaps he feels the same.
Lord, help me to overcome my pride.
Help me to apologize and let the
loving feelings win through.

167 Dear God,
When I'm feeling angry it feels as if I want to kill the
person, but I don't, because inside me there is
something that makes me calm down and forgive them.

Andrew O'Hara (aged 8)

168 Lord Jesus,
We get angry at so many things — our teachers, work,
friends and families.
Politicians make us angry, so do unemployment,
starvation and wars.
When we get angry we want to do something. That
can be good — but not when we want to strike out
and hurt.
Lord, help us to pray to you more when we are angry.
Teach us to be more tolerant of others. Let us
remember that harsh words and violence are not the
answer. Calm us with your peace and love.
Amen

Being Honest

Do not lie to one another.
Colossians 3:9

169 O Lord Jesus Christ, who art the way, the truth and the life, we pray thee suffer us not to stray from thee, who art the way, not to distrust thee, who art the truth, not to rest on any other than thee, who art the life. Teach us what to believe, what to do and wherein to take our rest.

Erasmus (1467–1536)

170 Dear Lord,
I pray that you will help me to be honest, and that you
will keep me safe from evil. When I talk, help me to
speak the truth and make me feel calm.
Amen

Peter Shepard (aged 10)

171 Father God,
Help us to tell the truth even when we are in the wrong.
I know it is hard, but please help us. Forgive us for our lies.
Amen

Danny Roberts (aged 9)

172 How happy is he born and taught,
That serveth not another's will;
Whose armour is his honest thought,
And simple truth his utmost skill!

Sir Henry Wotton (1568–1639)

173 When I open my mouth
Every word that I say
Paints a picture of me
For the others that day.

If I lie, all the colours
Are shaded with grey
And the light and the life
Fade away from the day.

If the words that I say
Are the truth then they see
A clear likeness of God
In the picture of me.

Being Obedient

Jesus went back with his parents to Nazareth
where he was obedient to them.
Luke 2:51

174 Dear God,
Jesus obeyed his mother in everything he did.
Help all children nowadays to obey their mothers
as Jesus did.
Amen

Lucy Stirling (aged 10)

175 Dear Father God, the most important thing of all is
that we are obedient to you, and I know that sometimes
I am not. Forgive me, Lord, when I disobey. Help me
to remember that I should do your will and not my
own. Help us all to be more obedient to our parents,
teachers and leaders.
In Jesus' name,
Amen

176 Lord,
If we obeyed your commandments the world would not
be in such a mess. Please help us to be more obedient
and help us to do the things *you* would like us to do.
Amen

177 Why do we find it so difficult to obey?
Why do we often want to break the rules?
Lord, help us to realize that rules and laws are made
for our own good — they are guidelines for how we
should behave.
If there were no laws everything would be chaos. When
we break the rules we often upset other people — so
please help us, Lord, to be more obedient.
In Jesus' name,
Amen

What About Tomorrow?

Jesus said: 'Do not worry about tomorrow,
for tomorrow will worry about itself.
Each day has enough trouble of its own.'
Matthew 6:34

178 Dear Lord,
You know what is best for us.
Help us not to worry about the future.
Because you love us all, you will take care of everything.

179 Dear Lord, I want to grow up to be a person who
absolutely loves and helps Jesus in every way.
James Lynch (aged 7)

180 What thou shalt today provide,
Let me as a child receive;
What tomorrow may betide,
Calmly to thy wisdom leave.
'Tis enough that thou wilt care;
Why should I the burden bear?

John Newton (1725–1807)

181 Dear God,

I am worried about the future. You know — the danger of that ozone layer and the pollution of the sea. I am worried about the oil and how much is left.

Lord, why do all these things have to happen? When will they stop? When will all the problems be solved?

James Pitcher (aged 10)

182 Dear Lord,

Please give children in generations to come a good world to live in. Give them clean air to breathe and fresh water to drink.

Sam Clements (aged 9)

183 I have life before me still
And thy purpose to fulfil;
Yea a debt to pay thee yet:
Help me, Sir, and so I will.

Gerard Manley Hopkins (1844–89)

184 Dear Father God,
May the future be good for everyone.
Let the world be patched up with goodwill
and let us pray to you more.
Amen

Lindsay Brewer (aged 11)

185 O Lord Jesus Christ our Maker and Redeemer, who
by thy providence hast made us what we are: thou hast
a purpose for us; do thou, O Lord, in thy mercy, fulfil
in us thy purpose. Thou alone art wisdom; thou
knowest what may benefit sinners such as we are; do
thou, in thy mercy, direct our future according to thy
will, as seemeth best in the eyes of thy Majesty, O Jesus
Christ, our Lord.

King Henry VI (1421–71)

186 Lord God,
I'm worried about the future because I think that the
sun will hit us one day. Will it?

Colin Fell (aged 10)

Sad Times

Listen to my words, O Lord, and hear my sighs.
Listen to my cry for help, my God and King!
Psalm 5:1-2

187 Help us through sad times, O Lord,
when we don't have joy.
Show us something funny to make us
happy again.

Jemma Harris (aged 12)

188 Please Lord, comfort those who are sad and grieving,
and those who just don't know which way to turn. Give
them courage to keep going although everything seems
to be hopeless.
Lord, when things go wrong it is then we realize that
there is only you. You are our hope and strength. We
pray that in their troubles and sadness more and more
people will come to know your love and peace.
In Jesus' name,
Amen

189 Stretch forth, O Lord, thy mercy over all thy servants everywhere, even the right hand of heavenly help, that they may seek thee with their whole heart, and obtain what they rightly ask for; through Jesus Christ our Lord. Amen

A Gelasian sacramentary

190 Dear Lord,
When I am sad and alone
I pray to you and then
I am not lonely any more.

Ashley Sturges (aged 12)

191 Dear Lord,
When we are sad you fill our hearts with happiness.
You are there with us and we won't forget that.
Just one chat always makes us feel happy again.
Thank you, for the things you do for us.
Amen

Tanya Hawker (aged 9)

192 Lord Jesus, you know what it is like to be sad
and worried;
please help us when we are troubled.
When we are anxious, give us courage to meet
our difficulties,
and to face whatever frightens us.
When we are unhappy may we be comforted,
knowing you are there.
Help us to bring all our worries to you,
because you understand.

Happy Times

Shout for joy to the Lord, all the earth.
Psalm 100:1

193 Dear God,
Thank you for giving us happy times. Help us to remember you when we are enjoying ourselves, and also those who don't have good times and aren't as well off as we are.
Debbie Herbert (aged 11)

194 Lord Jesus,
It was funny today. I got the giggles with my friend. Once we started to laugh we couldn't stop. We laughed and laughed until our sides ached. It was hilarious. I do feel good when I've laughed a lot. Thank you for inventing laughter.
Amen

195 Dear Lord Jesus,
Thank you for all the happy times I've had.
We would all like you back here on earth.
We want you to stop the wars.
Steven Lanes (aged 10)

196 Father,
When we are happy let us remember to share it with others. Help us to do our best to make others happy too. Thank you that there are times when we just feel so good that we want to sing for joy.
Amen

197 Lord,
help me to be happy always,
help me to be strong in you,
help me to be well all days,
help me to be good and true.
Amen

Ruth Hutchinson (aged 7)

Having Fun

God . . . generously gives us everything for our enjoyment.
1 Timothy 6:17

198 Dear Father God,
Thank you for sea and sand,
for rocks and rambles,
for pools and pebbles,
for shells and swimming,
for paddling and picnics.
I love the spray
and the foam,
the waves
and the splash.
Thank you for all the fun of the seaside.

199 Lord,
it was fun today
playing in the park.
We had a great game of football.
I scored a goal, Lord, it was brilliant!
Thank you for a good day.

200 BANG! A firework has gone off with a really loud
noise. HISS HISS CRACKLE ZOOM!
I wish that I could fly in the sky with all those colours.
Thank you, God, for all fireworks.
I like them.

Hannah Biddlescombe (aged 8)

201 Thank you for fun, Father —
for running in the summer rain
with no shirt on,
for speeding on my bike,
for climbing trees,
and playing tag.
For secret hideouts and passwords,
and all the other fun things to do,
thank you, Father.

The World Around Us

Our World

And God saw everything that he had made,
and behold, it was very good.
Genesis 1:31

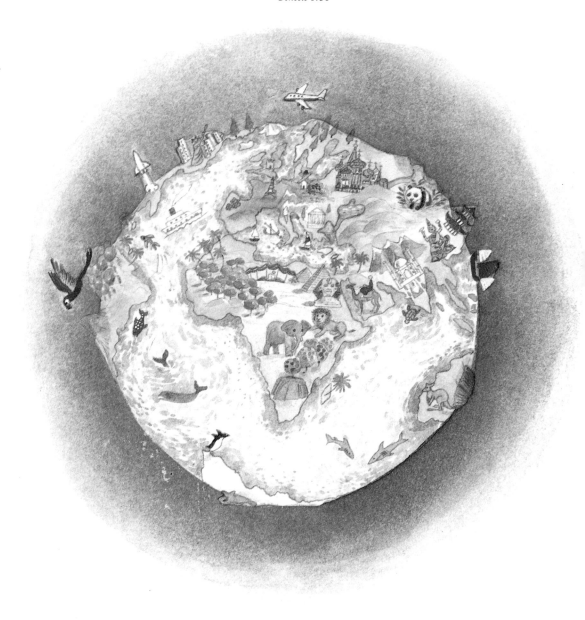

202 In the beginning there was darkness in the air
The earth was nothing
There was nothing there.

So God decided to have a bit of fun
And created the planets
And the sun.

He decided to call one planet Earth
And then this planet
Had its birth.

He made some darkness and some light.
He called light 'Day'
And called the darkness 'Night'.

He separated water from land
It was all done
By God's own hand . . .

And then the God Almighty, He
Created creatures
Of the sea.

And then made animals to roam
Across the Earth
Which was their home . . .

He then made people, Adam and Eve,
And with his help
They could achieve

Power over all living things
The fish with fins
The birds with wings.

Then on Sunday he had a rest
And that's the day
That I like best.

Alex D. Potterill (aged 11)

203 Dear Lord,
You made a beautiful world for us to live in.
Forgive us when we harm the things you created for us
to enjoy — the fresh streams and rivers, the trees and
green fields.
Help us to preserve and protect everything you made
and to stop those who selfishly destroy it.
Amen

204 Tonight I looked up at the clear, dark sky and saw
thousands of bright stars. How amazing that you have
made this wonderful world — it is so vast, Lord, yet
you love everything in it.
Thank you.

205 O God, great and wonderful who has created the
heavens, dwelling in the light and beauty thereof; who
has made the earth, revealing thyself in every flower
that opens; let not mine eyes be blind to thee, neither
let mine heart be dead, but teach me to praise thee,
even as the lark which offereth her song at daybreak.
St Isidore of Seville (560–636)

206 Thank you, Jesus, for your beautiful creation.
Thank you that you know where every bit of grass is,
every animal, tree and plant.
Thank you that you have everything under control.
Paul Scruby (aged 11)

207 We praise you, O God, for this lovely day — for the
blue sky, the warm sunshine, the flowers and tall trees.

208 Be thou praised, my Lord, with all thy creatures,
above all Brother Sun, who gives the day and lightens
us therewith . . .

Be thou praised, my Lord, of Sister Moon and the
stars, in the heaven thou hast formed them, clear
and precious and comely . . .

Bc thou praised, my Lord, of our Sister Mother
Earth, which sustains and hath us in rule, and
produces divers fruits with coloured flowers and
herbs . . .

Praise ye and bless my Lord, and give him thanks,
and serve him with great humility.

St Francis of Assisi (1182–1226)

209 Heavenly Father, we praise you because you have
created a world that is beautiful and awe-inspiring.
When we think about the size of the universe, or when
we hear the sound of crashing thunder or feel the
power of waves breaking on the seashore we remember
what a great God you are. And then we see the little
things like the pattern on a butterfly's wing, the
colours of the feathers on a duck, the different shapes
of leaves on the trees, and we realize that as well as
being a very powerful and mighty God, you also care
about little details, and have a great sense of beauty.
Please teach us to appreciate all that you have made and
to enjoy this world.
In Jesus' name,
Amen

Animals and Birds

So the man gave names to all the livestock,
the birds of the air and the beasts of the field.
Genesis 2:20

210 Animals in zoos, in films, in books;
hundreds, thousands, with different looks:
the monkey and the kangaroo,
the eagle and the cockatoo;
the tall giraffe, the crawling snail,
the tiny mouse, the giant whale;
the bear, the emu and the gnat,
the crab, the donkey and the bat.
Thank you for them, large and small,
thank you, God, who made them all.

211 We praise you, Lord, for the beautiful world you
made. We praise you for the animals and every tiny
insect. Teach us to treat all your creatures with respect
and kindness and to remember that you made them
and love them.
Amen

212 Dear Father, hear and bless
Thy beasts and singing birds,
And guard with tenderness,
Small things that have no words.
Anon

213 Dear Jesus,
I killed a spider today because it gave me the creeps.
Then I remembered that you made that spider, Lord,
just like you made me. I'm sorry.

214 Thank you, God, for animals,
for cats, dogs, tigers and bears.
Thank you for leopards and kangaroos.
Thank you God, for the birds that sing all day.
Amen

Abigail Williams (aged 6)

215 All things bright and beautiful,
All creatures great and small,
All things wise and wonderful,
The Lord God made them all.

Mrs C. F. Alexander (1848)

216 Lord,
We thank you for making so many wonderful animals
and insects — especially butterflies.

Mark Thomas (aged 10)

217 Little Lamb, who made thee?
Dost thou know who made thee?
Gave thee life, and bid thee feed,
By the stream and o'er the mead;
Gave thee clothing of delight,
Softest clothing, woolly, bright;
Gave thee such a tender voice,
Making all the vales rejoice?
Little Lamb, who made thee?
Dost thou know who made thee?

Little Lamb, I'll tell thee,
Little Lamb, I'll tell thee:
He is called by thy name
For he calls himself the Lamb.
He is meek, and he is mild;
He became a little child.
I a child, and thou a lamb,
We are callèd by his name.
Little Lamb, God bless thee!
Little Lamb, God bless thee!

William Blake (1757–1827)

218 Father God,
Thank you for all animals.
You created them with love, just as you created us.
Help us to protect them from those who treat them
cruelly and to look after them as you look after us.
Amen

219 Hear our humble prayer, O God, for our friends the
animals. We entreat for them all thy mercy and pity,
and for those who deal with them we ask a heart of
compassion, gentle hands and kindly words. Make us
ourselves to be true friends to animals and so to share
the blessing of the merciful. For the sake of thy Son,
the tender-hearted Jesus Christ our Lord.

A Russian prayer

The Countryside

The Lord is my shepherd, I shall not want.
He makes me to lie down in green pastures;
he leads me beside the still waters. He restores my soul.

Psalm 23:1-3

220 Dear Lord,
Thank you for all the lovely flowers and plants.
I think the whole world would be a flop without
the countryside. It is full of beautiful smells and
perfumes.
Thank you, Lord.
Amen

Henry L. (aged 10)

221 For flowers that bloom about our feet,
Father we thank thee.
For tender grass so fresh, so sweet,
Father we thank thee.
For the song of bird and hum of bee,
For all things fair we hear or see,
Father in heaven, we thank thee.

Ralph Waldo Emerson (1803–82)

222 Dear God,
Thank you for the sheep and pigs and cows.
Thank you for the fields — so very fresh and green.
Help us to preserve the countryside so that our children
can see it as we have.
Amen

Peter Gorell (aged 10)

223 Dear God,
Please stop me feeling sad about the birds that get
stuck in the awful oil leaks and are poisoned — and all
the other wildlife which suffers. I hope the pollution
will stop so that other animals can live in peace.
Amen

Michael Roberts (aged 10)

224 Father,
Help us to stop building all over the countryside and
spoiling it by dropping litter and cutting down trees.
Amen

Jamie P. (aged 10)

225 Dear Father God,
Please make me like the flowers — content to grow just
where they are, making the most of even the poorest
soil, yet bringing colour, brightness and pleasure to all
who see them.

Towns and Cities

The Lord said: 'Should I not be concerned about that great city?'
Jonah 4:10-11

226 God of all our cities
Each alley, street and square,
Pray look down on every house
And bless the people there.

227 Dear Lord,
There are so many lonely people in the city — people
we don't always notice among the bustling crowds. No
one seems to care about them. Lord Jesus, if there is
someone we know who is lonely, help us and our
families to overcome our shyness and to make friends.
Amen

228 Dear God, this is *our* town.
We think of its busy streets;
The cars and lorries, buses and bicycles;
The shops and the market;
Offices and public buildings;
Churches and chapels.
We think of parks and gardens
With trees and flowers;
Of birds and all wild creatures.
We think of thousands of people,
In many kinds of home . . .
And much more besides.
Dear God, this is *our* town;
Please help us to keep it nice.

229 The busy roads hum with the sound of traffic.
The pavements are full of people hurrying to and fro.
On trains and buses we see faces that are tired and
worried.
Everywhere there is noise, dirt, concrete, glass.
Lord, it is sometimes difficult to feel your presence
in the city.
Please bless those who live and work in large cities.
In the rush of the day, let them look up at the sky
and remember your beauty and love.

230 God of concrete, God of steel,
God of piston and of wheel,
God of pylon and of steam,
God of girder and of beam,
God of atom, God of mine,
All the world of power is thine!

Travelling

May the Lord keep watch between you and me
when we are away from each other.
Genesis 31:49

231 May the road rise to meet you.
May the wind be always at your back.
May the sun shine warm upon your face,
the rains fall soft upon your fields and,
until we meet again,
may God hold you in the palm of his hand.

An Irish blessing

232 Father God,
Please protect all those that we love as they travel.
Help them to feel your love with them as they go and
bring them safely home to us.
In Jesus' name,
Amen

233 Thank you, God, for the fun of travelling. Thank you
for jets and helicopters, liners and yachts, for rockets
and spacecraft, underground trains and escalators; for
cars and trains, scooters and lorries. Please watch over
all who travel today. Give them common sense and
politeness. Teach them to guard against accidents and
to obey the rules made for their safety.

234 Lord Jesus,
Please would you keep people in their cars safe.
Please protect my dad on the motorway.
Amen

Joel Harrison (aged 8)

235 Dear God,
How do you travel? My favourite ways of travelling are by flying and the train. Also, I can swim quite well in the sea.

Matthew Kane (aged 10)

236 Help me, Lord, to know that wherever I travel in your world, I cannot travel outside your care. Grant to those whom I entrust myself, the pilot, the engine driver or the ship's captain, a clear mind, a steady hand and the skills to do his job safely and well. For in trusting myself to their care, I trust myself to you.

The Weather

Praise the Lord from the earth . . . lightning and hail,
snow and clouds, stormy winds that do his bidding.
Psalm 148:7,8

237 I hear the wind and, dear God, I think of your Spirit.
I can't see the wind yet I know it's there by what it does.
It is very powerful.
It wakens me up, and makes me want to jump around.
I want your Spirit, Father, to be with me.

238 Dear Father,
Thank you for the good weather we have. We are very
lucky as we get the right amount of rain and sun so that
our plants can grow and we can have food. Please help
people in different parts of the world that don't have
good weather.
Amen

Melanie Murray

239 We plough the fields, and scatter
The good seed on the land.
But it is fed and watered by God's almighty hand.
He sends the snow in winter,
The warmth to swell the grain,
The breezes and the sunshine,
And soft refreshing rain:
All good gifts around us are sent from heaven above;
Then thank the Lord, O thank the Lord,
For all his love.

M. Claudius (1740–1815)

240 Dear God, we do not like the rain very much:
We get very wet sometimes on our way to school;
We cannot go out to play our games;
Sometimes it leaks into our homes or our school;
And sometimes it causes floods.
But we know that we need the rain:
We need it to make the crops grow;
We need it to provide water for drinking and
cooking . . . for washing and many other things.
We also remember what happens in lands where the
rain does not fall, where there are no harvests, no food
and nothing to drink except for water from wells.
So we say thank you, God, for the rain.

241 Lord,
The sun makes us feel so good!
Its light brightens up our lives.
Thank you for lovely sunny days and bright blue skies.
Thank you for the sun which warms us and helps
everything to grow.
You are like the sun, Lord. You warm us with your love
and help us to grow.
Let your light shine in our lives.
Amen

People Who Help Us

Help to carry one another's burdens,
and in this way you will obey the law of Christ.
Galatians 6:2

242 Go with the policemen each day, O Lord,
as they drive in their patrol cars
and break up fights
as they walk in dark alleys
and hunt in old houses,
looking for criminals.
Please keep them safe.
Help them make good decisions
when they arrest someone.
Teach them to love you
and ask you to help them in their work,
because a policeman's job is especially hard.

243 Thank you, Father, for doctors and nurses.
Thank you that we can go to them for help.
Thank you, also, for air and sea rescue teams
who help us if we are stranded.
Thank you, God, for people at church — that
we can go to them when we are troubled.
Thank you for all the people who help us.
Amen

Paul Coombes (aged 10)

244 Almighty Father, giver of life and health, guide and
help all those who are trying to make our roads safer.
Help those who drive and ride and walk on our roads to
be patient, unselfish and thoughtful of others, so that
everyone may travel in safety.

245 Dear God, we know how difficult it is to decide what is right, especially when some people may not be telling the truth. We ask your help for all those who are responsible for justice in our country: for ordinary people who form juries that decide whether a person is guilty; for judges and magistrates who must pass sentence; for judges who must judge between people who cannot settle their differences. We ask that all may be wise, sound and fair in their judgments and that justice may be done.

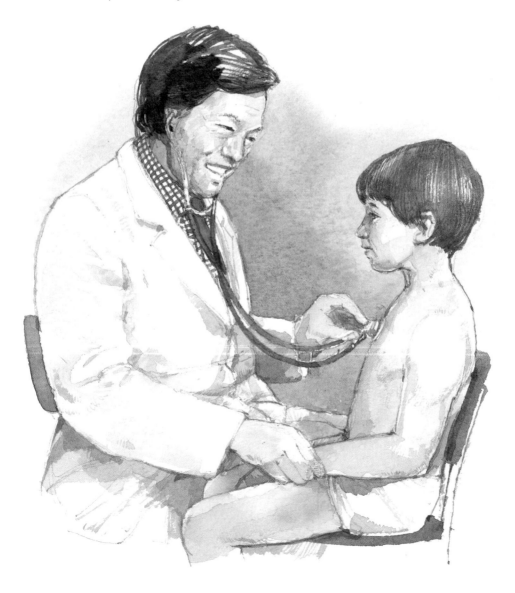

246 Father, thank you for firemen — for their courage and their constant care. When there is a fire we always expect them to be there, and often we forget the dangers they have to face. Lord, help us to remember that firemen have homes and families just like us. Bless and protect those who daily risk their lives for our sakes.
Amen

247 Thank you, Lord, for our parents and teachers who give their time so that we may learn about you.
Tracey-Anne Braye (aged 12)

248 Dear God, we pray today for the people whose work is dangerous: for those who build skyscrapers, bridges, tunnels and railways; for those who knock down old buildings or cut down enormous trees; for fishermen and sailors battling with stormy seas; for soldiers and airmen; for men in factories working with powerful machines; for coalminers, spacemen and circus people; for policemen, watchmen and firemen; and for all others who are in danger through their work. Please keep them from accident, we pray.
In Jesus' name,
Amen

249 Father,
Thank you for all the people who every day help us in some way.
Thank you for those who work in jobs which involve caring for others.
Thank you, too, for those who are just loving people who help out when and where they can.
Let us show our thanks by helping others ourselves.
Amen

People of the World

God loved the world so much that he gave his only Son,
so that everyone who believes in him
may not die but have eternal life.
John 3:16

250 We give thanks, O God, for your wisdom and love for all mankind. You have made people so different and yet so dependent on each other. Teach us to learn and to work together for the good of everyone; help us to learn about each other in our everyday lives, and to do all we can to foster peace and happiness among all nations, for we belong to your family throughout the world.

251 Lord,
I'm worried about people:
forgotten older people,
children without parents,
prisoners of war,
fathers without work,
people who have no homes,
who are hungry and cold,
or who live with problems
that wind up tight inside.
Show me how I can help
these other people.
Give me the right words
to tell them of your love.

252 I see white and black, Lord.
I see white teeth in a black face.
I see black eyes in a white face.
Help me to see persons, Jesus — not a black person
or a white person, a red person, or a yellow person,
but human persons.

Peace

The Lord will bless his people with peace.
Psalm 29:11

257 Creator of the world,
Help us love one another,
Help us care for each other
As sister or brother,
That friendship may grow
From nation to nation.
Bring peace to our world
O Lord of creation.

Translated from Japanese

258 Dear Lord,
Bless the leaders of the world today. Give them wisdom
and understanding and the courage to say what they
think is right. Help them in their decisions, so that this
world in which we live can have peace.
Amen

259 Thank you, God, for giving peace to this country.
Thank you that there are no wars here so that we can
have freedom to have a happy time.

Nadine Coombes (aged 8)

260 God, one of my teachers told us in class that in some
countries white people don't like black people. But the
Bible says that you made everybody in the world. So
please try and make people stop hating one another
and love one another instead. I believe that will stop all
the wars and bring peace.

A child's prayer from Liberia

261 O God, make us children of quietness and heirs of peace.

St Clement (1st century)

262 Father,
Help all the children who live in countries where there
is always fighting and fear.
Bless them, protect them and give them strength. Let
them know, Lord Jesus, that there is peace and comfort
in loving you.
Amen

263 O God, who art peace everlasting, whose chosen reward is the gift of peace, and who hast taught us that the peacemakers are thy children, pour thy peace into our souls, that everything discordant may utterly vanish, and all that makes for peace be loved and sought by us always.

A 5th-century Mozarabic sacramentary

264 Lord Jesus,
We pray for peace at all times. Whenever there is a war and nuclear weapons are flying about, we pray that people will have peace in their hearts.
Amen

Mark Thomas (aged 10)

265 Father God,
All over the world there seems to be trouble.
People are angry and full of hate so they bomb and kill each other.
Why can't they just stop and listen to you, Lord?
If only they knew that you are the answer.

266 Lord, make me an instrument of thy peace;
Where there is hatred, let me sow love;
Where there is injury, pardon;
Where there is discord, union;
Where there is doubt, faith;
Where there is despair, hope;
Where there is darkness, light;
Where there is sadness, joy.

St Francis of Assisi (1182–1226)

The Seasons

Spring

The winter is past; the rains are over and gone.
Flowers appear on the earth; the season of singing has come.
Song of Songs 2:11-12

267 We praise you, Lord, for the beauty of the spring.
We praise you for the new life all around — the
fresh, green shoots; the buds slowly opening and the
lovely blossom on the trees.
We praise you, Lord, for your promise of new life to all
that love and believe in you.
Amen

268 The daffodils
Wave in the wind.
God's pushing them.
The soft yellow petals,
petals like silk.

Darren Jones (aged 6)

269 How fresh, O Lord, how sweet and clean
Are thy returns! ev'n as the flowers in spring.

George Herbert (1593–1632)

270 Dear God,
Thank you for the springtime when all the birds have
their young. I like to see all the new animals — the little
calves and lambs. I like to watch them play and see the
young birds learning to fly. I really like the spring.

Michelle Belt (aged 9)

271 Thank you, Father, that spring is a picture
of your beauty.
Thank you for flowers and sunshine, and
that spring brings new life.
I pray that you would cleanse us, so that we
are fresh and new in you each day.
Amen

Kathryn Davies (aged 12)

Summer

O Lord, how manifold are thy works! . . .
the earth is full of thy riches.
Psalm 104:24

272 Dear Jesus,
Thank you that summer is here again;
For the joy of the warm sunshine and long days,
The green trees and fields and the bright flowers
everywhere.
Thank you for this time when all of nature seems to
praise your name.
Amen

273 Thank you, Lord, for the summer — the hot season.
Thank you that we can go on holiday and to the seaside.
We can swim in the sea and make sandcastles and have
lollies and ice cream on the beach.
Thank you for the fun of summer.
Amen
Lisa Scruby (aged 7)

274 We praise you, Lord, for the marvellous world in
which we live, and especially for the happiness of
summer; for the activities we enjoy and the freedom
which this season brings. May every moment be filled
with the joy of the knowledge of the love of our living
Lord. We ask this in his name.

275 For air and sunshine, pure and sweet,
We thank our heavenly Father;
For grass that grows beneath our feet,
We thank our heavenly Father,
For lovely flowers and blossoms gay,
For trees and woods in bright array,
For birds that sing in joyful lay,
We thank our heavenly Father.
Anon

276 Dear Lord,
Thank you for the summer
with the lovely hot sun
and the growing of the crops.
Glenda Witneyman

Autumn

God provides rain for the earth . . . he sends the wind.
Psalm 147:8, 18

277 Dear Father God,
autumn is a lovely season —
misty,
colourful and
bright.
The fruit is ripe and juicy.
The squirrels in the woods collect
nuts to feed them
through the winter.
Dew sparkles like diamonds
on early morning
cobwebs.
Thank you Lord, for this time.
Kelly Taylor (aged 12)

278 Now is the time for the days to grow shorter.
Cold breezes blow the leaves from the trees.
The earth is closing down for its winter rest.
All around are the glorious colours of autumn.
Lord God, we praise you for the beauty of the seasons
and that each one is special in its own way.

279 Thank you, God,
For the autumn when the leaves fall off the trees.
When I walk through the woods I like the sound
of the leaves going 'crunch'.
Amen

Michelle Belt (aged 9)

280 Father God, we are surrounded by the richness of the
colours of nature and the fruits of the harvest. Help us
to see these things as a reminder of your unfailing love.
Even as we pray, we remember how often we take you
for granted and sometimes even act as if you did not
exist. Forgive us for thoughtlessness and selfishness,
and help us to make this season a time when we resolve
to give you the very best that we can offer.

Winter

Lord God, it was you who set all the boundaries of the earth,
you made both summer and winter.
Psalm 74:17

281 Dear Lord, thank you that on cold
winter's nights I can go to bed,
tucked up warm, knowing that
you love me.
Amen

282 Dear Lord,
Please help all the little mice
and animals
survive the winter.
Amen

Tom Gregory (aged 12)

283 Winter is a time when it grows cold and things
freeze up.
Lord, sometimes my heart freezes up too.
When I am angry I can feel cold, hard and selfish.
I need your love to thaw me out, melt my heart and
fill me with joy again.
Perhaps that's how the earth feels when it is waiting
for the spring.

284 When the weather is cold, we say thank you God, for
our cosy homes, our warm school, and the warmth
within us that comes from the love of those around us.

285 Lord Jesus, winter is a time when the poor and old
people suffer more than ever. This winter, help us to
remember the people we know who may need some
loving care in the long, cold months. Let us make
sure they are keeping warm and have enough to eat.
Amen

Thanking God

Give thanks to him and praise his name.
Psalm 100:4

291 Now thank we all our God
With hearts and hands and voices
Who wondrous things hath done,
In whom his world rejoices.

M. Rinkart (1647)

292 Thank you, God, that you love us and care for us.
Thank you that we are able to praise you when we like.
Thank you that you are always there when we need
you, and that you always hear our prayers.
Thank you for helping us with our problems and that
you never go away.

Emma Ridgers (aged 13)

293 Thank you, God, for peace and happiness,
health and joy.
Thank you, God, for new life, plants and animals.
Thank you, God, for love.
Amen

Benjamin Harrison (aged 12)

294 Thou who hast given so much to me
Give one thing more, a grateful heart,
for Christ's sake.

George Herbert (1593–1632)

295 Father,
Forgive us when we forget to thank you.
We ask so much from you and expect you always
to answer our needs.
Forgive our selfishness, Lord.
Help us to be more thankful to you and to each
other, every day.
In Jesus' name,
Amen

296 Dear Lord,
Thank you that you sent your only Son to die for us.
Thank you for all the different people you made,
especially my friends and family.
Amen

Harry Lawson-Johnson (aged 8)

Praising God

'I will not be silent; I will sing praise to you.
Lord, you are my God, I will give you thanks for ever.'
Psalm 30:12

301 Let us with a gladsome mind
Praise the Lord for he is kind;
For his mercies shall endure,
Ever faithful, ever sure.

John Milton (1608–74)

302 Lord, we can praise you anywhere.
Thank you for what we learn from praising you.
Thank you that you bless us when we praise you.
Amen

Andrew F. (aged 12)

303 Whatever is true,
whatever is honourable,
whatever is just,
whatever is pure,
whatever is lovely,
whatever is gracious . . .
if there is anything
worthy of praise,
think about these things.

Philippians 4:8

304 Praise the Lord! Ye heavens adore him,
Praise him, angels in the height!
Sun and moon, rejoice before him,
Praise him, all ye stars and light.

John Kempthorne (1775–1838)

305 When I praise you, Lord,
I feel warm and bubbly inside.
Thank you that I am free to praise you!

Helen Garnham (aged 14)

306 My God, I thank thee, who has made
The earth so bright;
So full of splendour and of joy,
Beauty and light;
So many glorious things are here,
Noble and right.

I thank thee too that thou hast made
Joy to abound;
So many gentle thoughts and deeds
circling us round,
That in the darkest spot of earth
Some love is found.

Adelaide Procter (1858)

312 Dear Lord Jesus,,
Forgive me when I do wrong — when people say
comforting things and I turn them away.
Forgive me when I sin.
I will try to be like you.

Faith Harries (aged 8)

313 Father,
It is so difficult to forgive people who have hurt us or
our friends. We want to hit back — and sometimes we
do. But you taught us to love our enemies no matter
what they have done. Forgive us, Lord, when we do
not forgive others. Help us to understand *why* people
do and say hurtful things — and let our hearts be filled
with love for them.
In Jesus' name,
Amen

314 All that we ought to have thought and have
not thought,
All that we ought to have said and have not said,
All that we ought to have done and have not done,
All that we ought not to have spoken and yet
have spoken,
All that we ought not to have done, and yet have done,
For these words, and works, pray we, O God, for
forgiveness.

Traditional

315 Dear Lord,
Please forgive all the things that I have done wrong —
for hating people and things like that. I am sorry.

James Barclay (aged 9)

Graces

While they were eating,
Jesus took bread, gave thanks and broke it.
Matthew 26:26

321 Please bless this food,
Please bless this drink.
You're great, dear Lord
That's what I think.

322 God is great,
God is good,
Let us thank him for this food.
Amen

Anon

323 Be present at our table, Lord
Be here and everywhere adored.
His mercies bless and grant that we
May strengthened for thy service be.
Amen

Traditional

324 For your love,
For your care,
For your presence everywhere
We thank you Lord.
For our drink,
For our food,
For your gifts that are so good
We thank you Lord, in Jesus' name,
Amen

Chloë Bazlinton (aged 11)

325 Give me a good digestion, Lord,
And also something to digest;
But when and how that something comes
I leave to thee, who knowest best.

Part of a Refectory Grace, Chester Cathedral

326 Bless us, O Lord, and these thy gifts
which of thy bounty we are about to receive.
Through Christ our Lord.
Amen

Traditional

Special Days

Birthdays

So teach us to number our days
that we may get a heart of wisdom.
Psalm 90:12

331 Father,
Today it is my birthday.
Please give me a happy day — and also all the other
children in the world who were born on the same day.
Amen

332 Dear God,
I like birthdays even when they are not my own,
because everyone is happy. I like giving people
presents. At Christmas what do you celebrate most —
your birthday or Christmas?

Matthew Kane (aged 10)

333 For people and parties,
thank you, Lord;
for presents and cards,
thank you, Lord;
for games and songs,
thank you, Lord;
for cakes and candles,
thank you, Lord.

334 Thank you, God, for our birthdays.
But don't let us forget poorer people who don't even
know when their birthdays are, and certainly don't get
any presents.
Amen

Matthew McCormack (aged 12)

335 Our Father, we thank you for the greatest birthday of all when Jesus Christ was born. We thank you too for our own birthdays and for all that makes them happy days. As Jesus came to bring peace and joy to all the world, so may we help to bring gladness into the lives of others. For his sake.

336 Dear Father,
Today I am six and my
gran says she is sixty.
I know that you love us both the same,
though, Lord. Thank you.

Advent

Wise men came from the east to Jerusalem,
and asked, 'Where is the one who has been born king of the Jews?
We saw his star in the east, and have come to worship him.'
Matthew 2:1–2

Jesus said: 'I will come back and take you to be with me
that you also may be where I am.'
John 14:3

347 God our Father, we are getting ready for Christmas:
buying presents,
preparing for carol services,
rehearsing nativity plays.
We thank you for all the preparations you made for
the first Christmas:
through the prophets you told people to get ready
for Jesus:
you gave a baby, John, to Zechariah and Elizabeth;
you chose Mary to be Jesus' mother, and Joseph to
provide a home for them;
you called wise men from far away.
As we prepare to enjoy Jesus' birthday, make us
ready to listen carefully to the Christmas story and
to make room for Jesus in our hearts.

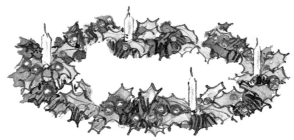

348 Father, we praise you for the joy of expectancy,
for waking in the morning to a sense of adventure,
for expecting to reach new targets in games or lessons,
for expecting to meet new friends,
for discovering new things to do, new skills to learn.
Father, we praise you for breaking through into our
lives when we least expect you.
We praise you for this season of Advent when our
expectancy grows into excitement as Christmas draws near.

Christmas

The angel said: 'I bring you good news of great joy for everyone.
Today the Saviour has been born.'
John 3:16

349 I'm so excited, Jesus!
Christmas is such a great time —
full of gifts and surprises.
But you were the biggest surprise of all
because no one thought you'd come
as a tiny baby
and be born in a poor place like a stable.
You were the best gift of all, too,
a gift from God to bring us life for ever.
Thank you for being the biggest surprise
and the best gift.

350 What can I give him,
Poor as I am?
If I were a shepherd,
I would bring a lamb;
If I were a wise man,
I would do my part;
Yet what I can I give him —
Give my heart.

Christina G. Rosetti (1830–94)

351 Dear Lord,
This Christmas please help those who will not get a
present or anything to eat or drink.
Please help those poor people as you did when you were
on earth, and help them to have a merry Christmas.

Tom Hetherington (aged 10)

352 Dear Lord Jesus,
Thank you for all the fun and games we can have at
Christmas. Thank you for my family and please help us
not to forget, amongst all the enjoyment, that
Christmas is really about celebrating your birth.

Matthew Irvine (aged 13)

353 Lord,
I'm so happy it's Christmas!
It's a time to remember you.
Please help me not to be selfish,
but giving.
Amen

Morgan Thomas (aged 8)

354 Dear Lord God,
Christmas often turns into a nightmare — a time when
my mum loses her temper, with all the rush. Instead of
a snatching, grabbing time let us enjoy Christmas as it
should be.
Amen

Lois Potter (aged 11)

ACKNOWLEDGMENTS

We would like to thank all those who have given us permission to include prayers in this book, as indicated on the list below. Every effort has been made to trace and contact copyright owners. If there are any inadvertent omissions in the acknowledgments we apologize to those concerned. Carol Watson has written and retains the copyright of all prayers except those acknowledged in the main text or listed below. Each figure refers to the number of a prayer.

Augsburg Publishing House: 56, 201, 242, 311, 347, reprinted by permission from *Lord, I Want to Tell You Something – Prayers for Boys*, Chris Jones, and 25, 103, 138, 251, reprinted by permission from *Just a Minute, Lord*, Lois Walfrid Johnson; all copyright © Augsburg Publishing House.   Ave Maria Press: 307, Joseph H. Champlin and Brian A. Haggerty.   Mary K. Batchelor: 159, from *The Lion Book of Children's Prayers*, Lion Publishing.   Basil Blackwell Ltd: 59, 225, 228, 240, 245, 284, 360, Rowland Purton, from *Dear God*, reprinted by permission.   Cadbury Ltd for 53, 81, 202, 268 from the *Cadbury's Fifth Book of Children's Poetry* © Cadbury Ltd.   Church Information Service: 120 from *Live and Pray* (first published 1970), Brother Kenneth CGA and Sister Geraldine CSA.   William Collins & Sons Ltd: 9, 19, 62, from *Prayers for Young People*, and 106, 337, 340, 364, from *More Prayers for Young People*, William Barclay, and 1, 92, 152, 210, 333, from *Let's Pray Together*, Geoffrey Marshall-Taylor.   Cassell plc: 100, from *The Junior Teachers' Prayer Book*, edited by D.M. Prescott.   Christopher Compston: 13, 26, 30, 33, 35, 176, 321, 331, 336, 359.   Dove Communications: 51, from *You Can Hear Him Listening* (published 1976), edited by Wendy Poussard and Shirley MacDonald.   Michael Ellis: 178, 281, 339.   Victor Gollancz Ltd: 50, from *Prayers and Graces*, Allen Laing.   Janet Green: 69, from *Home-made Prayers*, Lion Publishing.   William Heinemann Ltd: 252, from *Are You Running With Me, Jesus?*, Malcolm Boyd, and 257, from *Here a Little Child I Stand*, Satomi Ichikawa.   The Highway Press: 307, from *All Our Days*, I.C. Taylor and P.L. Garlick.   Hodder & Stoughton Ltd: 44, 58, 122, 135 from *A Patchwork Prayer Book*, Janet Lynch-Watson.   The Rev. Richard Jones: 230 from *Words to Share*, copyright © Richard Jones.   Christie Kenneally: 173 from *Your Kingdom Come*, Veritas Publishers.   The Lutheran World Federation: 37, 47, 260, Anza Lema from *Children in Conversation with God*, copyright © the Lutheran World Federation.   Jane Lucas: 136.   Marshall Pickering: 21, 118, 124, 146, 209, 253, Rebecca Harris, from *Junior Praise, Prayers and Readings*.   Nancy Martin: 127, 286. Also, 77, Graham Salmon: 244, Hope Freeman; 65, Nina Hinchy. All from *An Anthology of Prayers for Children and Young People*, Hodder & Stoughton Ltd, compiled by Nancy Martin.   A.R. Mowbray & Co. Ltd: 226, Joan Gale Thomas, from *God of All Things* (published 1948).   Joan Murray-Brown: 31.   National Christian Education Council: 95, 250, 274, 280, 348, from *Prayers to Use With 11s–13s*; 90, 236, 343, from *Prayers to Use With Young People*; 80, 85, 88, 91, 192, 255, 256, 347, 361, from *When You Pray With 7–10s*; and 346, Lilian Cox, from *New Child Songs*. Used by permission.   Estate of Ogden Nash: 12, from *Parents Keep Out*.   Scripture Union Publishing: 144, from *Let's Talk to God*, 142, 233, from *Let's Talk to God Again* and 248, from *Prayers for Children*, all by Zinnia Bryan. Also, 198, from *My Book of Prayers*, Helen Gompertz.   Donald Soper: 75, from *The Piccolo Book of Prayers*, Pan Books Ltd.   St Paul Publications: 237, Anthony Bullen, from *Fifty Prayers for Young People*, copyright © St Paul Publications (UK).